Th[illegible] Self

Gnostic and Jungian Foundations of Modern Identity

Jeffrey Satinover, MD
Pastoral Care Ministries

GROVE BOOKS LIMITED
BRAMCOTE NOTTINGHAM NG9 3DS

Contents

'Tell us pleasant things, prophesy illusions.
Leave this way, get off this path,
and stop confronting us with the Holy One of Israel!'
Isaiah 30.9-12

FOREWORD

Dr Jeffrey Satinover is an American Jungian Psychiatrist with a Jewish background, who in recent years has come to faith in Christ and has found a spiritual home in the work of Leanne Payne. As a result he has begun to reflect critically and Christianly on the Jungian view of human existence in general, and the nature of the true self in particular.

The material which follows is the groundwork he has done in this area. In a culture which has very often bought into a Jungian psychology this comes as a refreshing challenge, not least to much Christian counselling which has been significantly shaped by Jung. What he has to say also addresses the whole Christian approach to spirituality which is also greatly influenced by Jung's thinking.

In this work, Dr Satinover acknowledges his indebtedness to Jung, and identifies what can rightly be affirmed in the work that he did. However, he also uncovers the long process of the development of the notion of self-identity from the Renaissance and Leonardo da Vinci to the present day, and offers a pointed critique of it.

I welcome this work, not as the last word on the subject, but rather as a voice, in strongly Jewish accents, calling Christians to lay hold afresh of the wholesome Hebraic understanding of personhood in the midst of many contrary and confusing voices.

Many Christians, and particularly those in counselling and spiritual direction, will find much to enlighten and challenge in this work.

Robert Warren

The Cover Illustration is by Peter Ashton

First Impression March 1995
ISSN 0144-171X
ISBN 1 85174 287 5

1
Leonardo da Vinci and the Priesthood of Self

One of the great problems we face today is the peculiar development and nature of modern selfhood. For modern man, personal identity does not develop around a core sense of God's presence in our souls, but in his at-least-seeming absence. There was a time when, wondering whether selfhood even had any real basis, I had become fascinated by the figure of Leonardo da Vinci. I was in good company. For Leonardo had been an object of similar interest to Freud—and to many other psychoanalysts as well.

In keeping with his view that *all* aspects of human psychology were ultimately traceable to erotic frustrations of various kinds, Freud had tried to show that Leonardo's immense creativity arose out of an underlying homosexual conflict which he was unable to face as such. A 'turn,' as it were, into creativity was the way that Leonardo dealt with unacceptable homosexual impulses caused by his ambivalent feelings toward his mother. Leonardo apparently never enacted his illicit sexual impulses, but neither did he attempt to develop romantic relations with women. According to Freud, he kept women at a distance by maintaining a highly idealized image of them that conflicted with their earthly reality. This image was expressed in the idealized women of Christian iconography that so dominated his painting, and especially by the enigmatic, unapproachable *Mona Lisa*.

Leonardo's Childhood 'Memory'

The centrepiece of Freud's analysis was a 'memory' Leonardo claimed to have recalled from childhood:

> *'[W]hile I was still in my cradle, a vulture came down to me, and opened my mouth with its tail and struck me many times with its tail against my lips.'*

To a psychoanalyst, the fact that Leonardo did not question the authenticity of his (clearly implausible) 'memory' suggests that it was linked to highly conflictual themes which he was reluctant to face squarely. The tail in Leonardo's mouth Freud saw as relating directly to homosexual proclivities. Unable to acknowledge his desired-yet-feared sexual impulses, Leonardo could experience them only in disguised form, and by placing them in the past. The 'memory' was merely a screen for his unacknowledged, 'latent' homosexuality.

Freud based this quintessentially psychoanalytic interpretation not just on the obvious analogy suggested by the image of a bird deliberately placing its tail in Leonardo's mouth (and flapping it back and forth), but also on the fact that *the bird in question was a vulture*. Freud constructed a long, really quite brilliant, explanation that linked Leonardo's homosexuality to the fact that the vulture was an ancient Egyptian mother goddess—Mut. Freud demonstrated how Leonardo's homosexuality and ambivalence toward women (at once idealizing them and keeping them at a distance) arose from his painfully ambivalent relationship with his mother, and from the fact that he was raised much of the time by his grandmother.

Freud thus pulled an image entirely out of its context in Egyptian mythology, with all its various pagan connotations, and applied it willy-nilly to Leonardo. And yet its application to Leonardo seemed to have a certain uncanny appeal, for lurking in the background of Freud's paper—and in the minds of his many well-educated European readers—were all those well-known connections: between homosexuality and 'mother's boys'; between creative brilliance and *fin de siècle* decadence; between dissipated youth and voluptuous death (one thinks immediately of Thomas Mann's *Death in Venice*). The vulture, indeed, as pagan Great Mother Goddess of life and death, brooding over the children whom she shall soon smilingly eat, seemed to fit perfectly.

And furthermore, shortly after Freud published his article, Oskar Pfister, a Swiss pastor turned psychoanalyst, discovered the most amazing thing: in Leonardo's 'Madonna and Child with St Anne'—mother and grandmother—the folds of the women's dresses created the perfect shape of a vulture!

In most eerie fashion, the discovery seemed to confirm deep psychological connections in Leonardo's psyche between his ambivalence toward his mother and an ancient Egyptian mother goddess. One might well wonder how such connections might arise. Is there, perhaps, a shared, timeless dimension to the psyche that manifests itself in such imagery?

The Psychoanalytic Plot Thickens

Perhaps not. For it turns out that the German translation of Leonardo's notebooks upon which Freud was dependent was faulty. The bird—a *nibbio*—was not a vulture at all, but a kite, which is a species of falcon.

The psychoanalysts persisted nonetheless. Thus Erich Neumann, Jung's most prominent disciple, claimed that the vulture was *symbolically true for Leonardo* even if the literal connection was nonexistent! (In fact, the vulture more accurately could be described as a fantasy *in Freud's mind*—and subsequently in Neumann's—than in Leonardo's. We know much more about Freud's complicated relation with his mother than we know about Leonardo's with his.)

Neumann did, however, make a change in his interpretation of the meaning of the vulture. Rather than understanding it as symbolizing Leonardo's attachment problems to his actual mother(s), Neumann, following Jung, saw it *as a symbol of a (psychically) real Mother Goddess—the mother 'archetype'—standing behind, as it were, Leonardo's creative genius*. In the terminology that the medieval alchemists applied to themselves (Gnostic, heretical Christians upon whose work Jung based much of his own), Leonardo was 'an age-old Son of the Mother'. Jung also referred to himself in these terms. It was this archetype, this goddess, who so filled Leonardo with genius—at the cost of his earthly passions.

It took sixty years for any psychoanalyst to come to terms with the simple fact that the bird was no vulture. James Hillman, a neo-Jungian whose work in many ways purifies Jung of any residual bourgeois, Swiss, Christian traditionalism, brings out in stark detail Jung's fundamentally Gnostic belief-system. Hillman, too, related the bird to Egyptian mythology, but not to the vulture-goddess Mut. The bird was rather Horus, sun and divine falcon, child of Osiris the *Father*.

Implicit in all previous analysts' interpretations was the accusation that Leonardo was neurotic: a 'momma's boy' of one sort or another as evidenced by, among other traits, his homosexuality. Hillman's argument was an impassioned defence against this accusation. These interpretations, he argued, with their presumption of illness, whether viewed personally (as in Freud) or archetypally (as in Neumann) represent *the forced imposition of a single set of values and standards upon a man whose spiritual genius and individual uniqueness was so profound that he left all bourgeois restrictions behind him*—on sexuality as much as in his art, and especially in his vaunting ambition to be the first man to fly. Leonardo was no neurotic boy of mother, human or divine; he was the divine soaring son of the Great Father Spirit.

Greatness as Divinity

As the man who almost did fly, as the man whose genius defined the very term, 'Renaissance Man', as the man whose imagination soared truly beyond the confines of his age, Leonardo belonged not to 'the Mother archetype', Hillman argued, but to the archetype of 'Divine Eternal Youth', the eternally rising god of the sun. In Leonardo's unique genius, in his variant of personal identity, death, eternal youth and transcendent imagination came together in a way that constitutes not just an exception to the mundane, but more than that. In Leonardo we directly witness *the only god there really is: human greatness*. As William Blake was later to put it in *The Marriage of Heaven and Hell*:

> 'The worship of God is honouring his gifts in other men, each according to his genius, and loving the greatest men best. Those who envy or calumniate great men hate God, *for there is no other God...*'

for:

> 'All things are comprehended in their Eternal Form in the Divine Body of the Saviour, the True Vine of Eternity, the Human Imagination.' *(A Vision of the Last Judgment)*

Leonardo was the very prototype of modern identity formation—identity rooted in personal grandeur. Leonardo's homosexuality, in this view, was almost a necessary concomitant of his genius, and this is a motif that forms a subtle undercurrent to much of today's romanticization of the connection between homosexuality and creativity.

Paganism and Polytheism

In the 1800s, Shelley averred that 'Poets are the unacknowledged legislators of mankind', capturing the essential conceit that undergirds the myth of the 'suffering artist': 'I suffer not because of anything for which I am responsible, but because I am not understood, and I am not understood because of my unrecognized greatness.' Hillman agreed and justified this Jungian restructuring of modern identity, by saying, in effect: 'There are many kinds of people and each type is governed by a different god. Each therefore has his own kind of sexuality, his own style of relationship, his own method of gaining fulfilment in work. You cannot judge a man, especially a gifted man, by the standards of one god; certainly not by the bourgeois, patriarchal standards of the so-called "God of Israel." *Stop confronting us with the Holy One of Israel*, for we are such men as will burst the bonds of all monotheistic tyranny. Leonardo and we, his many modern simulacra, are an elite, priests of Horus, the falcon-god.'

Thus the *great* individual is mythologized and resymbolized into the new ideal, replacing the *good* individual, his character flaws redefined as virtues by placing them within the frame of reference drawn by a different 'god.' All that is needed for full self-acceptance in the modern mode is to identify the correct frame of reference, hence the proper altar at which to sacrifice.

In this way the door was opened to a resurgence of pagan—which is to say, polytheistic—ways of assessing and valuing human behaviour. We are not all subject to the same law of God; there are a variety of different moralities to which we may be subject, depending on to which 'god' we belong.

Traditionalists have cogently argued that this kind of moral reasoning is no advance, but will surely lead us to the worst immorality of the past. The abortion of children reconceptualized as waste-products of purely sexual liaisons is, of course, already widespread. Paedophile groups within gay activism in the English-speaking countries are even now preparing to soften public opposition to child-adult sex as it has already largely succeeded in doing in Holland. The worship of the murder of 'life not worth living' (*unlebenswertige Leben*, not so long ago a despised component within Nazism's organized adulation of 'pagan youth') is now slipping across the border of acceptability by appealing to our sympathy for the ailing aged. This is the vulture as 'mother-goddess': sex and death in a sanctified embrace.

Is it far-fetched to posit so direct a connection among the Renaissance origins of self-worship, modern moral relativism and the influence of Jung on current, wholly self-referential forms of identity? Consider the following comments about the goddess Artemis (a favourite figure in Renaissance iconography) by the prominent Jungian analyst Ginette Paris in her book, *The Sacrament of Abortion*:

> 'It is time to call back the image of Artemis, the wild one, who...chooses to belong only to herself...[t]he Artemis myth manifests itself in our lives...by a...movement away from...fusion with others, the most extreme example of fusion being the connection between a mother and her young children. Artemis...invites us to retreat from others, to become autonomous.'
>
> 'Our culture needs new rituals as well as laws to restore to abortion its sacred dimension...I've heard women address their fetus directly...and explain why it is necessary to separate now. Others write a letter of farewell and read it to a friend, a spouse, or indeed to their whole family. Still others invent their own farewell ritual, inspired perhaps by rituals from other cultures, like offering a little doll to a divinity as a symbol of the aborted fetus...[T]he pro-lifers see the spiritual dimension but keep it imprisoned within official orthodoxies, as if no other form of spirituality existed. What if my religious beliefs are pagan?'

An Appeal to Facts

Both Freud's classic and Neumann's Jungian psychoanalyses of Leonardo's bird-fantasy founder on the simple fact that a *nibbio* is not a vulture but a falcon. But Hillman's switch from 'vulture' to 'falcon' is equally tendentious, for the simple reason that there is no connection *whatever* between Leonardo and Egyptian mythology. Hillman's reconstruction merely tracks the fading influence of classical psychoanalysis in favour of quasi-theological psychologies such as Jung's (and his followers) that meet the modern hunger for 'spirituality' in a way that exacts no moral cost.

To invent their respective psychoanalytic mythologies, all these analysts had to avert their eyes from the basic facts available to art-historians. One day, Leonardo was watching a flock of kites wheeling in the sky and he became intrigued by their extraordinary manoeuvrability, typical for birds of prey who attack their victims in mid air. (Vultures eat only creatures that have ceased moving, on the ground.) Making careful sketches, he noted how:

> '...by waggling their tails back and forth they turned swiftly now this way, then that, thus steering themselves as a pilot turns a boat.'

Suddenly, he turned over his sketch of the kites and their waggling tails and hastily scribbled his 'memory.' It would have immediately been understood by his contemporaries as saying something quite specific about Leonardo himself.

As the Renaissance proceeded, the concern with personal greatness rapidly spread. In the Middle Ages, monks and masons could toil for generations on a single illuminated manuscript or a great cathedral, and no one would ever know of them. The individual author or artist was of no account—*Soli Deo Gloria*: to God alone belonged the glory.

Indeed, because the glory was God's it was possible for projects to be carried out over centuries, yielding an attention to beauty, to craftsmanship and to loving detail as impossible to us today on spiritual grounds as would have been photocopiers and skyscrapers to medieval man on purely technological grounds. But in the Renaissance all this changed. Authors and artists began to sign their works; the pride in personal greatness slowly began to displace the greatness and glory of God.

And with all this concern about greatness, about being 'a Renaissance Man,' there arose a distinctive conceit: that one was marked out for greatness early in life, predestined to one's role. The mark of this future greatness was typically as follows: *while still an infant, wild animals enter one's mouth and leave, without harm.* Thus, of Ovid it was said that *while he was an infant, a swarm of bees entered his mouth and left without harming him.* And so he was fated to be a great poet, with words like honey. In Leonardo's own library were at least five books recounting similar such tales. In short, Leonardo's 'memory' was a Renaissance cliché.

To fly was the never-to-be-achieved ambition of Leonardo da Vinci's life. What Leonardo was saying therefore, perhaps knowingly, perhaps unwittingly, to his peers—and to himself—was that *'I, Leonardo, greatest of all men, am destined to fly!'* Sadly, this mark of greatness he was concerned to have others acknowledge and appreciate.

But, of course, he was not destined to fly. Alongside whatever reasonable level of interest he had in the problem of flight, Leonardo was possessed by a degree of compulsion. In other words, his intense desire to fly, his need to think of his success as anointed by the gods and have others think so as well, was a *narcissistic* configuration. He had invested his identity in the idolatrous worship of personal greatness. On the altar of that idol Leonardo sacrificed much of value. He was notorious for his slipshod preparations in other domains; his 'Last Supper' is nearly gone because of it.

At about the time during my study of Leonardo when I was approaching this conclusion, I had the following dream:

> *Leonardo appeared before me. His chest was opened in the way that portraits sometimes show Jesus with his chest open to expose his heart; or show an individual whose chest is opened there to reveal Christ within. So in this dream Leonardo's chest was open to view, and there in the place of his heart—or of his God—was a figure enthroned. Who? Leonardo himself!*

Here was the terrifying portrait of modern selfhood: God stripped out of our core that we might seek our identity in self-enthronement. Here was the secret vice that so attracts us in our idolization of the 'Renaissance man,' of he who seeks identity in accomplishment and personal stature. The emptiness, the essentially frozen isolation of a heart devoid of God, was in that dream made perfectly clear.

At that moment, the enchantment had been broken; all romanticization of the Renaissance, or of Leonardo, was at once dispelled. I understood that at that brilliant moment of history we so admire, there entered into the West a dark spirit—mixed with, sometimes disguised as, light—whose bitter sowings we all now reap.

The Resymbolization of the Western Psyche

This dream points, as well, to the central resymbolizing act that has so swiftly overtaken and corrupted the Western imagination, and which now provides a theology for so many of our divinity schools and seminaries. The original template for the symbol in my dream is that of the human spirit animated by the spirit of God residing within it—incarnational reality, whose great exemplar is, of course, the Messiah. The dream illustrates the resymbolization of this sacred image into its modern variant. In this version *God is replaced by self, self is enthroned in the position of God.*

Such is the 'new' religion of the age. So prepared are we for it that had I presented this dream out of context, it would have been easy to offer it as a vision not of the ancient Hell, but of a modern, new-age, Heaven: 'This is the next stage in human evolution. We are now past the primitive projections of our own psyche onto a non-existent divine realm. Illumined, we now know that ultimate reality is found within, our very own Selves. The great promise of the ancient bringer of light, Lucifer, the serpent-god of Wisdom, in our time nears fulfilment: soon we shall indeed be as gods.' There are other examples of resymbolization. But this is the father of them all: the psychological transformation of God into self.

Resymbolization in Jung

Freud's interpretation of Leonardo's vulture is an instance of 'resymbolization,' especially as it has been propelled forward by psychoanalysis. As the Judaeo-Christian tradition has weakened, spiritually-starved people have progressively replaced the very specific symbol system of the Bible, upon which Western civilization is founded, with various mostly Eastern and pagan imports. The vulture, for example, nowhere appears in the Bible as a symbol of the mother goddess, nor of anything else. Indeed, in the Bible, *the 'mother goddess' herself is but a symbol,* a creation of humanity's fantasy life, which, when treated as real, becomes 'an idol of wood and stone' embodying godless humankind's enslavement to his natural impulses—especially those of untrammelled sexuality and violence. Hence the universal, dual nature of 'mother goddess' imagery: sex and death; fecund and destructive.

A particularly striking instance of this resymbolization in Jung's life—it must have been prompted by his familiarity with Christian symbolism—can be found in his dreams. In his autobiography, *Memories, Dreams and Reflections*, Jung reports a repeating dream that ushered in a period of great personal distress when he feared he might become psychotic:

> 'In the third dream [of mine] frightful cold had again descended from out of the cosmos. This dream, however, had an unexpected end. There stood a leaf-bearing tree but without fruit (*my* tree of life, I thought) whose leaves had been transformed by the effects of the frost into sweet grapes full of healing juices. I plucked the grapes and gave them to a large waiting crowd' [italics mine].

Compare this with Revelation 22.2:

> 'On each side of the river stood the tree of life...And the leaves of the tree are for the healing of nations.'

This dream marked the beginning of the process out of which Jung developed a psycho-theological system which was to become his contribution to the modern worldview. When, years later, his project was complete, he again had a vivid dream of a great tree. The tree was bathed in light in the centre of a city square in Liverpool. He again identified it with the tree of life in Revelation with its streams of living water ('Liver' means 'life'; 'pool' means 'water', he noted).

Both dreams do clearly depend upon the tree of life imagery in the the Book of Revelation. But in Revelation, the tree of life belongs to no one person (it is not 'John's' tree of life). Jung's personalized reinterpretation is the prototype for the kind of 'resymbolization' that has led many others to interpret prophetic, spiritual symbols in a personalized, psychological fashion. Indeed, this is the essence of the Jungian resymbolization: the replacement of the divine by the self; in Jung's own choice of terminology, by the 'Self.' The Messianic elevation of self implicit both in Jung's dreams and in the theories that he developed out of them is implied, too, by the identification of 'Jung's tree of life' as the healing *vine* ('sweet grapes'). We will see later that Jung's elevation of self to godhood (including his own self) was part and parcel of the 'new' religion of self he was developing.

Good and Evil

Here is another resymbolization: the transformation of *evil* into *wisdom*. This resymbolization is certainly widespread today—it is another way of speaking of moral relativism—but it would be wrong to consider it uniquely modern or in its essence merely philosophical. It is a quintessentially *spiritual* deception and an ancient one indeed. Indeed it is the *original* resymbolization of God's reality, the one first proposed to humankind—alas, successfully—by the serpent, concerning his own nature.

In the Bible, the serpent is not so much wise as cunning. It is he himself who implies that his cunning is the same as wisdom. He is nonetheless intelligent, even extraordinarily so. But in the Judaeo-Christian tradition, his gifts notwithstanding, he remains the unequivocal symbol of evil. Because he is cunning, what he presents to man is not pure falsehood, but rather, *a mixture of truth and falsehood*. It is this that makes his words so seductive.

In ancient Gnostic symbol systems, as also in the dreams, fantasies, and visions out of which arose Jung's personal iconography, the serpent is the symbol of 'higher' wisdom. He is therefore the one who brings 'enlightenment'. Hence one of his names is 'Lucifer', meaning 'the light-bringer.' He enables mortal man to transcend good and evil—or so he tells us—by incorporating them into a 'larger' whole. Indeed, it is he who *invents* the very notion that the world and its destiny can be understood by perceiving it as divided into opposites that move dialectically toward some higher synthesis. Spiritual progress therefore consists of moving beyond these opposites to positions of ever more transcendent superiority.

As the creature 'more subtle than any beast of the field,' the serpent therefore appeals to our grandiosity in his claim, 'Ye shall not surely die: for God doth know that in the day ye eat thereof, then your eyes shall be opened, and ye shall be as gods, *knowing good and evil*.' (Genesis 3.1-5) The Hebrew is better translated as 'deciding for yourselves what is good and what is evil.'

The displacement of God by self is therefore also the loss of a clear, revealed vision of good and evil. How can a mind ultimately driven by natural, selfish instincts possibly generate, on its own, a vision of perfect goodness? The godly ideal is alien to mere nature, and cannot arise out of it. In Robert Browning's words, 'Man's reach must exceed his grasp, else what's a heaven for?' In our creaturely limitations we can only imperfectly embody good, even when we have been shown and acknowledge what it is. Thus we always end up as a composite of good and evil, and so nature, that which simply is (the seen real) may point to but can never replace the revelation of what should be (the unseen real). This is the essential fallacy of nature worship and 'goddess theologies' that redefine the creation as divine.

The vision of the *holy* is, as it were, the star that we cannot touch but which points the way. To follow this star is to stand firm in the knowledge that God is wholly good. This is basis for conscience, for the ability to discern, in the midst of life's complexities, good from evil, and to separate them to the greatest extent possible. The material world in its fallen state is *always* composite, both good and evil. No person is ever wholly evil nor wholly good, nor is any act. To seek the Lord's good within a fallen creation is therefore to be pressed ceaselessly to discern. For the man of faith, the primordial vision of goodness that the Lord himself has established is itself the truer reality than the one in which we dwell. Heaven has a greater substance, as it were—is more *real*—than the impure, composite experiences of 'real' life.

God's vision of the good is one wherein *evil is nothing but God's absence,* it is not his coequal. Hell is the *total* absence of God as heaven is his total presence; earthly hells are his relative absence as earthly heavens are his relative presence. To the extent that we are present to God, we are not to our fallen selves; to the extent we are absent to him, we are present to those selves only.

This idea that, for all its power, evil is substanceless is well-known to orthodox Christian theology as the *privatio boni*—evil as the mere 'privation of good.' It is equally part of orthodox Jewish theology. Thus:

> '...one must realize that true perfection is God's essence. Every fault is merely the absence of his good and the concealment of his presence. The closeness of God and illumination of his presence is therefore the root and cause of every perfection that exists. The concealment of his presence, on the other hand, is the root and cause of every fault, the degree of deficiency depending on the degree of this concealment.'[1]

Consistent with his Gnostic reinterpretation of Christianity, Jung attacked the *privatio boni,* insisting that evil (Satan) is on a par with good (God). He argued that the *privatio boni* allowed people to take evil less seriously. Yet precisely the reverse is true, as evidenced by the nature of Gnostic morality (as will be discussed) and by Jung's own fascination with, and blindness to—until it was too late—the dangers of the Nazi embrace of paganism.

Masculine and Feminine

As we have progressively abandoned the eternal, unseen Divine standard in favour of a sequence of transitory, visible, fallen ones, our capacity to discern good from evil, truth from lie, has diminished. In like fashion the discrimination between the true feminine and the true masculine has been lost. Human beings, as individuals or as groups, are inevitably a mixture of masculine and feminine qualities, as of good and evil ones. No one is purely masculine or purely feminine. But now we have lost the ability to distinguish these qualities and rightly value them. The result has been a widespread disordering of relations between men and women. And because the relationship between man and woman is the basis of the family, the destruction of the family is progressing rapidly. Western, Judaeo-Christian civilization is not the only culture to have understood this truth. The ancient Chinese, for example, understood it well:

> 'The *Family* shows the laws operative within the household that, transferred to outside life, keep the state and the world in order.'

1 Rabbi Moshe Chaim Luzzato, *Derech HaShem (The Way of God).*

The importance of the family structure is equally obvious from a sociological point of view. There is a vast body of research which makes it clear that, although far from perfect, the traditional family structure is associated with the lowest levels of psychopathology and with the highest levels of human happiness and accomplishment. A society in which there is a large proportion (there can never be 100%) of stable, traditional families—that is, with a mother who remains permanently married to a father both of whom are their children's first and only parents—will produce the highest percentage of relatively healthy individuals. The smaller the proportion of such families, the higher the rates of alcoholism and drug addiction, suicide, homosexuality, pornography, promiscuity, and crime. Even physical health is profoundly affected by the presence or absence of stable family structures.

What these studies do not attempt to prove is that a proper relationship to God is the linchpin of family stability. The research does reveal, however, that those social subgroups with the greatest reverence for the family—such as the Amish Christians in America and the Hasidic Jews worldwide—have the most stable families, and the basis of that reverence is faith in God.

Psychological Spirituality: The New Gnosticism

The ultimate foundation of family stability is the recognition that 'God is light, in him there is no darkness at all.' Deep beneath such fine-sounding (and in their place genuinely good) terms as 'tolerance', 'diversity' and 'inclusiveness' lurks the Gnostic idea that darkness can be incorporated with light into a 'new' and 'superior,' more *psychologically realistic* image of God. In the words of a prominent Jungian analyst and minister of divinity:

> 'Jung...would look with approval on...the psychological understanding of the doctrine of atonement...moving...to a more balanced view of mixed good and evil within the natural and spiritual orders...Grace, concomitantly, is seen as less utterly transcendent and more closely woven into the natural order.'

Is this 'new' psychotheology in fact still Christian, as maintained by Jung's many proponents in ministry? The author continues:

> 'What Jung foresaw as a possible future for Christianity...would in many ways be continuous with Christian tradition, but also be very different from it. Jung's concept of Christianity's transformation is on this order: [that]...Christianity and its authoritative source book, the New Testament, would become for the transformed version of the tradition what Judaism and the Old Testament became for Christianity, a prefiguration and forerunner of *the new revelation*.'[2]

As early as the 1940s, Jung's improved God-image ('the Self') included within

2 Murray Stein, *Jung and Christianity: The Psychotherapy of a Religious Tradition* pp 184-186 (italics mine).

it not only evil, but matter and 'the feminine', on the grounds that these are a kind of 'lower trinity' excluded from the Godhead by 'the patriarchy.' These motifs have now all found their way into modern 'Christian' theologies in the form of the worship of nature [matter] ('the Earth is God's body') 'inclusive-language' liturgies and 'goddess-worship' [the 'feminine'], and tolerance of 'alternate lifestyles' (invariably meaning a variety of extramarital and perverse sexualities [evil]); in short, *the world, the flesh and the devil*.

This ancient, resurgent Gnostic identification of a supposedly higher, paradoxical 'Wisdom' with both 'the Feminine' and with pansexuality has re-emerged in modern attempts within mainstream denominations to generate a new theology that places 'Sophia' on a par with God (as a kind of goddess-consort to a male YHWH); or to consider Sophia as the feminine 'part' of the godhead. Thus at 'Re-imagining' (note the emphasis on imagination) a recent major conference co-sponsored by the national leadership of the 8.7 million-member United Methodist Church and the 2.7 million-member Presbyterian Church USA, conference organizers and speakers offered a near-total transformation of Christian ritual and theology, including such examples as:

- With outstretched arms, conference participants called on *Sophia*, the Greek personification of wisdom found throughout ancient Gnostic, Hermetic and alchemical texts, to bless each speaker.
- 'Our maker Sophia,' they prayed, 'we are women in your image; with the hot blood of our wombs we give form to new life. With nectar between our thighs we invite a lover, and with our warm body fluids we remind the world of its pleasures and sensations.'
- The conference emphasized finding the divine in oneself and in nature.
- To cheers and laughter, the Revd Barbara K Lundblad, pastor of Our Saviour's Atonement Lutheran Church in New York City, proudly announced, 'We did not last night name the name of Jesus. Nor have we done anything in the name of the Father and of the Son and of the Holy Spirit.'

To call Gnosticism 'Christianity' is to stretch the meaning of both to the point of absurdity. In the words of another speaker at the 'Re-imagining' conference:

> 'We will shed the excess baggage of patriarchy and assume the interwoven stance of a people doing justice or we will die trying. Whether it is Christian or not is frankly, darling, something about which I no longer give a pope.'

2
Gnosticism

'Heresies perish not with their authors, but like the river Arethusa, though they lose their currents in one place, they rise up again in another.'
Sir Thomas Browne *Religio Medici* (17th Century)

'Modernism is the synthesis of all heresies.'
Pope Pius X (20th Century)

The Greek *gnosis* simply means 'knowledge'. The essential appeal of Gnostic thought lies in its claim that *salvation may be attained through secret knowledge* available only to an initiated elite. It is an approach to spirituality closely linked to the Greek mystery religions of the centuries just before and after Christ, heavily influenced by the doctrines of Babylon and India.

A Gnostic variant of 'Christianity' was roundly attacked both by Paul and by John. The whole of 1 John is essentially a polemic against Gnostic 'Christians' who had already emerged from among the very earliest circles of believers. Likewise, Jewish criticism of Gnostic Jews was then, and has remained, equally pointed. Indeed, John's own harsh attacks on 'Jews who are not Jews' were aimed not at Pharisees as is commonly taught, but at Samaritan synagogues which had imported the Babylonian mystery religions and syncretized them with Judaism. The seductive strength of Gnosticism allowed it to spread swiftly among pagan populations more inclined to season their sins with mysticism than to abjure them with repentance.

In time, Gnosticism became the major heresy battled by some of the early church fathers. But alas, those fathers not battling it, were all-too-frequently embracing it—just as today.

Gnostic 'Christianity' is notoriously intellectual and spiritualized (as one might imagine for a system which claims that salvation may be acquired via knowledge). And yet, historically, cultures in which Gnostic thought have taken root tend strongly toward the licentious (again, just as today)—a seeming contradiction.

We see this distinctive two-sidedness in alchemy, a later variant of Gnosticism projected onto chemical transformation, which was the major focus of Jung's researches. The chief figure of alchemy was its *spiritus familiaris, Mercurius*, known as *duplex* (duplicitous). He was closely allied to and sometimes overtly identified with the devil because of his slippery, trickster-like nature. (Our word 'devil' is cognate to the German *zweifel*, meaning doubt, literally 'two-cased.') For the alchemists, as for all Gnostics, duplicity is not a vice, but a higher virtue, representing a 'union of opposites'. The spirit *Mercurius* is likewise identified with the Greek god *Hermes* (Hermes is Greek; Mercury, Roman). Hermes is the presiding spirit behind both Hermes Trismegistus, the apocryphal Egyptian founder of alchemy, and behind antique Hermetic Philosophy. As this series of interconnections already suggests, the historical variants of Gnostic thought are but the visible eruptions of a single, underground current.

Gnostic 'Salvation'

As briefly noted above, the basic principle of Gnosticism is that 'salvation' is achievable through one's own mental activity (often thought of today as higher *imagination;* recall Blake's comments above). Gnosticism makes a subtler, more mystical, appeal than either 'faith' or 'works': that ultimate value is itself a mental state, and that mind is capable, on its own, of achieving it ('only eat this...and ye shall know...').

The esoteric nature of Gnostic systems, their restriction to an 'elite', runs directly contrary to God's plan of salvation which, is of course, available to everyone equally, as is his love. 'Come near me and listen to this: From the first announcement I have not spoken in secret; at the time it happens I am there' (Isaiah 48.16). The seductive, rarely-acknowledged, attraction of all esoteric 'initiations' is precisely that only an elite have it. As a narcissistic aspect of our fallen nature, we all want to be a part of an elite—'ye shall be as gods!'

The Reconciliation of Good and Evil

However the different stages of initiation are purportedly marked, the innermost circle of all Gnostic systems is *a mystical vision of the reconciliation of good and evil*. The transcendent achievement—Gnostic salvation, enlightenment, Luciferic illumination—is defined as that which stands beyond the mere opposites, the primordial ones being good and evil.

The vision of good and evil in a supposedly 'higher' union creates the spiritual foundation for relativized standards of personal behaviour. In the Judaeo-Christian worldview, creation exists primarily as a field in which man lives out a struggle to make good manifest against its absence, in spite of his final inability to do so on his own. It is not a world whose purpose is determined by physical laws, although these hold it together. In the Judaeo-Christian view, ultimate reality is *moral,* and holiness is the fundamental characteristic of its creator. The vision of a union of good and evil—and the standards that emanate from such a vision—can have but one result: the false prophet becomes progressively uncoupled from the basic truth of reality and increasingly ensnared by desires that are exclusively materialistic. For if his vision of reality—and of the ultimate purpose for human existence—is false, in time material satisfaction will be all that is left him.

In pursuit of its hopeless aims Gnostic philosophy soon justifies freedom from all constraint. In the end, the Gnostic stands alone, encircled by inflamed, unsated desire. The vision at the innermost circle of initiation is in fact the innermost circle of hell, because there is no place outside the *hell of self* where good and evil can successfully be united.

Historically, Gnosticism begins in ascetic intellectualism. Within a few generations its followers degenerate into licence, since the instincts can never be constrained by mere intellect, let alone by falsehood. Instinctive gratification soon becomes identified with spiritual progress, the whole process of degradation being dressed-up in lofty-sounding rhetoric. When, after the French revolution, the goddess Reason was enthroned in Paris (at *Our Lady*), it was a prostitute who was paraded through the streets to be crowned. In the same way today's intellectuals everywhere in academia and schools of divinity now dignify with fancy language that which, in an earlier age, would simply and unself-consciously have been named as depraved.

The goddess-worship that has insinuated itself into Western religious practice is but a predictable consequence of our seduction by Gnostic ideologies. By whatever name, it is but the ancient Canaanite goddess Ashtoreth—with her retinue of sacred prostitutes, male and female, and her endless production of disposable children, by-products of untrammelled sex-worship—who is repeatedly re-enthroned during eras of apostasy, as much today in the decaying centres of Christendom as before in Israel of old. For those with eyes to see, the youthful-seeming goddess is an ancient crone indeed.

Moral relativism, in-group snobbery, sexual licence masquerading as spiritual superiority—all these motifs are well-captured in the following epigram favoured by the ancient Gnostics:

> 'Whosoever being *of* this world has intercourse with woman shall not attain to the truth because he has so acted under the power of concupiscence. But whosoever being *in* this world (yet not of it) does *not* so love a woman as to obtain possession of her, is not of the truth, nor shall attain to the truth.'

Superspirituality and Atonement

The 'new' religion that reconciles opposites is linked as well to a view of history which is non-incarnational, non-sacramental and super-spiritualized. Gnosticism views history (personal and national) as merely 'material'—which, in a funny way, is to say 'immaterial'—while viewing 'spirit' as entirely divorced from the world. On the other hand, the Judaeo-Christian tradition views history as the concrete enactment of a divine Providence for and in the world.

The new vogue word for this segregated world of spirit is 'imaginal,' a neologism meant to avoid the potentially derogatory word, 'imaginary.' Though somehow real, this 'imaginal world' is seen as unrelated to the physical world, and hence not to be judged by its effects. Through 'imagination' we enter this 'world' to find meaning free from moral obligation. Gnostics thus are at once free to despise the world and to indulge in it.

By contrast, the Bible is the story of God's working *in history*. The symbols that are present in the Bible are not *only* symbolic, subject to endless interpretation, nor only mythic, describing events that occur in another realm. They are *also* historical events. It is their tangible reality that inspires faith; their symbolic reality that engenders meaning. Hence the obvious fact that devotees of the 'higher criticism' are for the most part faithless. The Lord says 'feed my sheep,' but a purely mythopoetic view of the Bible is spiritual saccharin: intensely sweet, but nutritionless; poisonous in high doses.

Who were the Gnostics who had emerged from the earliest Christian circles? They were adherents to the new sect who would not accept the historic reality of a resurrection, and so in various ways used it as a spiritual metaphor, finding analogies to pagan myths of dying and reborn gods. But primarily, *they were people who refused to accept that salvation required substitutionary, atoning sacrifice,* the central message of both Old and New Testaments.

In Gnostic systems, old and new, substitutionary atonement has no meaning whatsoever except as a rather gory metaphor. Thus Jung, too, reduced the significance of the cross to the idea that in a crisis, one is 'suspended between the opposites' and is therefore, so to speak, 'crucified'. (A more pedestrian, if equally gory, figure of speech, is 'to be impaled on the horns of a dilemma'.) In this spirit, at the 'Re-imagining' conference cited above, the Revd Delores S Williams, a professor at Union Theological Seminary in New York City, eloquently declaimed:

> 'I don't think we need a theory of atonement at all. I don't think we need folks hanging on crosses and blood dripping and weird stuff.'

Jung's Explicit Redevelopment of Gnostic Spirituality

From its position within early Christianity, the Gnostic thoughtline moved forward to the Manichees, by whom Augustine was seduced for a time. The Albigensians, who got their start during the reign of the Merovingians, established a Gnostic Christian state in the south of France. Their influence may still be felt in the sanctified extramarital romances of the 'Courtly Love' tradition and in Grail Mysticism. (The quest for the Holy Grail has long been interpreted by 'esoteric Christians' as a thinly disguised allegory for the stages of occult initiation.) After Manichaeism was successfully conquered by the church, Gnosticism dove underground to rise up again in allegorized form within alchemy. From alchemy, it went to the Knights Templar and thence to all the other quasi-occult groups of secret initiates that sprang up in the middle ages in pursuit of the Holy Grail. When the Templars finally declined, the early Masonic societies arose. When these lost their essentially mystical character to become political king-making machines (stimulating and powerfully affecting the course of the French Revolution), the Gnostic stream moved to the occult groups and spiritualistic societies of the nineteenth century, most of whom expressly traced their ancestry back to Gnostic roots.

This has roughly been the course of the river Arethusa that ever 'loses its current in one place only to rise up again in another'. Though in his epigram Sir Thomas Browne refers to heresy in general, he is suggesting a hidden, more specific, meaning. Arethusa is a (mythic) river said to start in Greece and dive under the sea to rise up again in Sicily. But its origin in Greece is Arcadia, the land in which occultists claim their great 'Hermetic mysteries' have their primordial source.

That Jungian psychology is the pre-eminent modern variant of Gnosticism would come as no surprise to Jung—nor would he consider the label a derogatory epithet. On the contrary, he devoted most of his adult life to a study of alchemy. He explicated both antique Hermeticism and the 'Christian' Gnostics. His earliest writings were about spiritualism. And he assigned his wife, Emma (and one of his prominent female students, Marie Louise von Franz) the task of explicating the Grail legends. Jung openly considered depth psychology in general—and his in particular—to be a modern reawakening of Gnosticism which he actively promoted as superior to Christianity. Jung was keenly aware, as well, of his own world-historical significance, perceiving himself as the prophet of a 'new dispensation' that would be carried forward by his school.

Within the world of Jungianism since Jung, Gnostic and pagan strains have moved ever more forcefully to the fore. Because he still wrestled with his Christian background and forebears (his father was a pastor), Jung's own work displays rather a mixture of Gnostic, pagan and genuinely Christian motifs. His followers, however, have clearly evolved an informal consensus that the Christian elements in Jung are mere residue. It is the purely Gnostic and pagan elements which are now advanced vigorously, restrained only fitfully by the requirements of clinical professionalism. *The Sacrament of Abortion,* cited above, is an example of how explicitly pagan religious practices are being promulgated within the Jungian movement as a basis for psychological 'health.'

The Serpent's Promise

Neither is it surprising that in Jung's own internal life—as in Gnostic mythology and iconography—the image of the *serpent* looms large as the bringer of his 'enlightenment.'

As his friendship with Freud collapsed (upon whom he described himself as having 'a religious crush'), Jung underwent a powerful series of spontaneous visions to which he himself attributed *all* his later ideas. Jung describes their onset as follows:

> '...I had the feeling that I was in the land of the dead...I caught sight of two figures, an old man with a white beard and a beautiful young girl. The old man explained that he was Elijah, and that gave me a shock. But the girl staggered me even more, for she called herself Salome!...Elijah assured me that he and Salome had belonged together from all eternity...They had a black serpent living with them which displayed an unmistakable fondness for me...According to Gnostic tradition, Simon Magus went about with a young girl he had picked up in a brothel. Her name was Helen and she was considered the reincarnation of Helen of Troy.'

Recall that John the Baptist, 'in the spirit' of the prophet Elijah and forerunner to the Messiah, was beheaded by the corrupt and vicious Salomé. Elijah, too, had to deal with a corrupt and lascivious female ruler of Israel, Jezebel. The idea that Elijah and Salome, of all people, 'belonged together from all eternity' (like Simon Magus and Helen of Troy) is a gloss, therefore, on the Gnostic conception that good and evil are both part of one superordinate, eternal whole, embodied in the cliché of lecherous guru and lewd seductress.

Close analysis of these visions of Jung, placed in the context of his letters to and from Freud (as well of the complicated erotic entanglements then present in the psychoanalytic milieu from which Jung had just fled), presents an entirely different, rather more mundane, dimension to this vision, with its at once lofty yet crudely erotic 'spirituality.' 'Elijah', the Jewish prophet, is clearly a reference to his estranged mentor, Freud (whom Jung characterized in writing as 'an Old Testament prophet') and 'Salome' possibly to Lou-Andreas Salomé, the beautiful, brilliant courtesan-turned-psychoanalyst. Reputedly the most beautiful woman of her age, she was the consort of numerous European intellectual luminaries, Rilke and Nietzsche among others and had apparently just spurned Jung's attempts at friendship—or more—in favour of Freud. Of course, if Freud with his psychoanalytic gospel was Elijah the forerunner, then Jung, Freud's 'crown prince and heir', bearing his Gnostic gospel, must be...?

As I mentioned before, the use of the serpent as a guide to 'wisdom' is a classic example of the resymbolization of our Judaeo-Christian heritage. In that heritage, the serpent is the God-given image of cunning evil. In Gnostic mythologies, it has been resymbolized into an image of higher wisdom and enlightenment. This serpent of 'illumination' first makes his appearance early in Genesis, of course, at the Fall. For the Fall is indeed directly associated with *gnosis*—knowledge. There, his *only* effort was to present humanity with a seductive lie pertaining to the value of a certain kind of knowledge; the lie was seductive because it was so plausible.

Paganism and Polytheism

Note, too, that the Hebrew of Genesis 3 says, 'Ye shall become as *gods, (elohim)*' not 'Ye shall become as *the* LORD *(Yahweh)*.' We have already seen some connections between Gnosticism and paganism; the former is a sort of theological substrate of the latter. But paganism is also *polytheism,* which stands in utter contrast to the monotheism of the worship of the Lord.

It is polytheism that stands behind the mantras of 'diversity', 'tolerance' and 'inclusivity' now being so widely misused. The modern, psychologized manifestation of polytheism is the plausible idea that *since people differ, there must be different standards of behaviour—hence of morality—to apply to each type of person.* In polytheism there is no absolute overarching standard toward which all people need aspire. For each type of person, there is *a god* among the many gods. There is a god for the tribe of women (who is herself a goddess), there is a god for the tribe of warriors (who is himself warlike), there is a god for the tribe of homosexuals (who is himself pansexual), as though we are not all under one God and obliged to one law.

Psychology, Polytheism and the Worship of Instinct

Psychology tends toward polytheism because, as a matter of practice, it often must remain neutral toward people's behaviour. But this general principle does not always hold, even within the clinical domain proper. Do we approve of the neutral psychotherapist who helps a passive individual with murderous urges overcome his passivity? But there is worse. When a neutral psychology becomes the authoritative worldview then an empty, inflated self with relativized values and relativized standards of behaviour—polytheism—will swiftly become the new religion, as indeed it already has, whether recognized as such or not.

In polytheism, ancient or modern, each group has its own god. In Jung's view, these are the *spiritual faces of the instincts,* which he named 'archetypes'. 'The archetypes are the images of the instincts' he says. 'Archetypal images' arise in our minds to represent important, common, human configurations. Thus there is a Warrior archetype, a Great Mother archetype (for example, the vulture goddess above), a Father archetype and so on, for each of the major 'situations' of human life. Each archetype is the image of an underlying instinct. In other words, the 'gods' of polytheism are merely the images of our own instinctive drives. The pagan psychotheology that lurks behind Jungianism, and that has spread so widely within the church, is simply *the psychologized worship of instinct.*

Pagans make, and worship, idols that are mere representations of their own impulses—'gods that are no gods'—gods of power, money, fame, violence and sexuality. In primitive societies, these idols are of wood and silver and stone; in civilized ones they are of words and concepts—an insignificant difference. In paganism, people worship at different altars because each has a different dominating instinct.

The instincts are 'nature within,' the counterpart of 'nature without'; both God-given and -created. The instincts are thus a major part of our creaturely existence, to be honoured as part of God's creation, and to the extent we are able, placed in his service. This means to use them as *he* wishes, not necessarily as *we* wish, for 'our bodies are not our own.' We are not to worship them in his place.

We must not worship nature not only because it is not God, but also because all of nature—whether within or without—no matter how beautiful, is fallen. Psyche (not to be confused with spirit) is linked to the brain. It is a manifestation of nature. A morality which attempts to derive itself purely from psyche, with reference to nothing beyond, will end up being either overtly amoral (as with reductionistic psychologies deriving from Freud), or polytheistic (as are those spiritualistic psychologies that derive from Jung).

The Judaeo-Christian story, throughout both Testaments, can be seen as a relentless battle between God—*the* God—and all other forms of 'spirituality'. Gnostic ideology, for all its lofty pretensions, is thus directly linked to licence. A Gnostic 'Elijah' truly does belong with Salome. But 'licence' is merely a shorthand term for *pagan* spirituality whose dominant feature is an orgiastic fertility worship. Thus, the earliest 'Gnostics' were simply the Baal-worshippers of Canaan. And indeed, we find condemned in the Old Testament not only the fertility and goddess-worship of the Canaanites (along with their sacrifice by fire of the unwanted 'products' of their fertility rites), but their 'occult,' secret-knowledge practices as well: divination, astrology and 'sorcery,' the original meaning of which was the use of drugs to produce a heightened state of 'consciousness.'

3
The Effect on Public Morals: A Warning

In the years following World War I, Jung applauded what he considered a pagan awakening in Germany, marked by the renewed worship of nature, romance of the German *Volk* and youthful high spirits. By contrast to the lusty young Germans who took to the fields and highways with their backpacks, singing songs of praise to the ancient pagan gods, he saw Judaeo-Christian culture as weak and moribund (professionally, he regarded what he called 'Jewish *psychology*' particularly problematic). In an interview on Radio Berlin as late as 1933 he was still citing Hitler, and he noted with approval the distinctive need of the more 'youthful' German nation for a *Führer.* In 1936, he wrote:

> 'But what is...piquant to a degree is that an ancient god of storm and frenzy, the long quiescent Wotan, should awake, like an extinct volcano, to new activity, in a civilized country that had long been supposed to have outgrown the Middle Ages. We have seen him come to life in the German Youth Movement, and right at the beginning the blood of several sheep was shed in honour of his resurrection. Armed with rucksack and lute, blond youths and sometimes girls as well, were to be seen as restless wanderers on every road from the North Cape to Sicily, faithful votaries of the roving god...The Hitler movement literally brought the whole of Germany to its feet...and produced the spectacle of a nation migrating from one place to another. Wotan the wanderer was on the move.'

Only very late in the 1930s did Jung come to repent of his enthusiasm for the emerging Nazi ideology, because he had begun to see that its manifestations were not so salutary as he had thought. But he never ceased romanticizing the pagan gods, longing as he did for the mystical dimension he considered them to embody. He continued—presciently:

> 'Wotan must, in time, reveal not only the restless, violent, stormy side of his character, but also his ecstatic and mantic [divinatory] qualities—a very different aspect of his nature. If this conclusion is correct, then National Socialism will not be the last word. Things must be concealed in the background which we cannot imagine at present, but we may expect them to appear in the course of the next few years or decades. Wotan's reawakening is a stepping back into the past; the stream was dammed up...But the obstruction will not last forever...the water will overleap the obstacle.'[3]

3 *Collected Works* Volume 10 pp 180,192.

Yet Heinrich Heine, the German Jewish poet from the mid 1800s, was more far-seeing, and far more realistic about what a reawakening of paganism would bring. His words tell us precisely what awaits us should we persist in our worship of pagan deities in whatever guise. He wrote the following more than one and a half centuries ago:

> '...should ever that taming talisman break—the Cross—then will come roaring back the wild madness of the ancient warriors, with all their insane, Berserker rage, of whom our Nordic poets speak and sing. That talisman is now already crumbling, and the day is not far off when it shall break apart entirely. On that day, the old stone gods will rise from their long forgotten wreckage and rub from their eyes the dust of a thousand years' sleep. At long last leaping to life, Thor with his giant hammer will crush the gothic cathedrals. And laugh not at my forebodings, the advice of a dreamer who warns you away from the...scientists. No, laugh not at the visionary who knows that in the realm of phenomena comes soon the revolution that has already taken place in the realm of spirit. For thought goes before deed as lightning before thunder. *There will be played in Germany a play compared to which the French revolution was but an innocent idyll.'*[4]

The Demonic

The sheep sacrifices alluded to above by Jung have always been ignored by modern historians with their relentlessly materialistic view of human nature. But these sacrifices were, in fact, a prelude to the human sacrifices that were soon to follow. Nor was this development merely one of sheer brutality. It was the expression of a self-conscious, explicit, diabolically-informed occult-mindedness that key members of the Third Reich deliberately invoked and cultivated. The Third Reich actually established a special ministry for occult affairs. Good reason to consider carefully the true nature of the forces with which our own *Kulturführer* are now so blithely tampering.

Psychology recognizes the existence of what are called *complexes*. The term has come into general usage but it originated with Jung. Early on, as a result of studies involving his cousin, who was a medium (or 'channeller'), Jung recognized that the human psyche was capable of dissociating. In extreme cases, dissociation can take the overt clinical form of *multiple personality disorder*, but Jung realized that some degree of dissociation was normal.

Our seemingly unitary personalities are actually composites of 'sub-personalities' each embodying a cluster of interrelated feelings, emotions, attitudes, behaviours, ideas and—crucially—*consciousness*. Each complex experiences itself subjectively as *the* personality, most easily seen, again, in

4 *The Works of Heinrich Heine* Volume V pp 207-209.

trance- or possession-states, as well as in multiple personality disorder, but in varying degrees true of everyone.

In a generally well-integrated person the exchange among parts of the self is fluid and nearly invisible; only keen observers will detect their autonomy. In highly imaginative individuals, the lines of dissociation may be made quite visible, as displayed in their creative work. Think of a novelist, for example, whose various characters represent aspects of his own personality. Furthermore, in psychopathological conditions, claimed Jung, the personality either never achieved synthesis, or has lost it, and so the parts of the self are separate and on vivid display.

In his doctoral thesis concerning his cousin, the medium, Jung claimed that the spirit personality which possessed her was actually a dissociated part of herself—indeed, a *superior aspect of her personality* of which she was consciously unaware and which she never accepted as herself.

As a theory of spiritualism, this 1902 formulation is consistent with modern theories concerning 'spirit personalities' in multiple personality disorder. Secular clinicians would concur that when a person sincerely seems to be a 'channel' for a spirit, all that is occurring is the emergence of a dissociated sub-personality, with nothing supernatural to it.

But Jung was being disingenuous. His fascination with the occult went considerably beyond the idea that spirits were mere parts of the self. Indeed, after submerging it during his affiliation with Freud, Jung's original interest in the occult re-emerged, albeit in formulations meant to preserve Jung's keen interest in being perceived as 'scientific.'

What Jung did was to sanitize his occult and spiritualistic ideas by recasting them in scientific-sounding language. For example, the reading of omens he reformulated as 'the perception of meaningful coincidences' based on the 'a-causal relatedness of events' for which he invented the term 'synchronicity,' phrases that *feel* scientific. But a careful study of Jung's writings reveals that he has no scientific explanation for such a concept. It remains as far from the world of science as does 'divination.'

More importantly, we find the same thing to be true when we carefully examine his full description of complexes, archetypes—here is the crux of the matter—*in their relationship to so-called parapsychological phenomena* ('synchronicity' among them).

Jung started by defining 'complexes' as normal sub-personalities within the human psyche. He continued by pointing out how an *archetype* forms the nucleus, as it were, of every complex. Since each archetype is merely the 'image' (representation in consciousness) of its underlying instinct, this is to say that every complex develops around an instinct. The instincts are inherited; the complexes 'flesh out' the instinct with actual experience, so to speak. It is the individual differences in the configuration of instincts from one person to another, combined with differences in life experience, which results in the individual 'personality.' Personality tends to fall into typically recurring patterns because there are pre-existing 'dividing lines' between the archetypes that tend to repeat themselves. So far there is nothing supernatural about this model of the psyche; indeed, there is much about it to commend.

Jung then took his model further, providing examples of archetypal images (personalities) from mythology, religion and fairy tales—but still not introducing anything supernatural. We noted that Jung's archetypes are what the ancients referred to as 'gods.' If anything, his view (so far) of (pagan) religion is rather appropriately reductive. For it says, in effect, 'Those ancients who spoke of 'gods' were merely projecting their own complexes onto an imaginary metaphysical screen.' And indeed, up to this point, Jung's model of the brain-based psyche remains compelling and useful.

But Jung pressed it a critical step further. He claimed, first, that *parapsychological phenomena genuinely existed* and second, *that such phenomena were typical accompaniments of an 'activated' archetype*. Interestingly, both Freud and Jung were somewhat in agreement as to the reality of parapsychological occurrences. But it was Jung who related them to complexes and archetypes, and who followed through on the implications of that connection. For Freud they remained oddities which he preferred to ignore. So convinced was Jung of the value of the occult, however, that at a crucial early meeting with Freud he became quite agitated by his then-mentor's resistance to the subject. In the midst of their argument, Jung felt as though his abdomen were 'becoming red-hot'. Suddenly there erupted a loud noise, 'like a gunshot.' Jung announced to Freud: 'There, that is...a *catalytic exteriorization phenomenon*' (a recently-coined 'scientific' term for what had always been understood as the tricks of a *poltergeist*, literally, a 'rowdy spirit'). Freud replied, 'Oh, come, that is sheer bosh.' Jung replied, 'You are mistaken, Herr Professor. And to prove my point I now predict that in a moment there will be another.' And there was. It turned out that a centuries-old, long-since thoroughly-dried piece of wood had inexplicably shattered in a nearby drawer—twice.

Let us examine what follows from Jung's scientific-sounding proposition that 'activated archetypes generate parapsychological events.' When an instinct is activated—aggression, or sexuality, or hunger, or the drive for nurturance, and so on—one of the basic animal cravings is aroused and we find ourselves driven in accord with its dictates. Associated with the subjective sense of craving (or desire or intent) is a measurable physiological arousal. The 'parapsychological phenomena' somewhat more common in this state of instinctive/archetypal arousal encompass the supernatural moving of objects at a distance without physical force ('telekinesis', an example of which is Jung's 'catalytic exteriorization phenomenon') and the supernatural transfer of information ('telepathy,' 'precognition'). Typically, these events occur in fragmentary, unreliable, fashion.

As with 'synchronicity', the terms 'parapsychology', 'telepathy,' and 'telekinesis' are but neologisms that *relabel* a class of events for which *there exists no scientific explanation.* Parapsychology research, such as it is, merely continues to demonstrate that its subject matter exists.

There is, however, an older explanation for such events. This older view holds that 'parapsychological' phenomena are not entirely psychological, but at least in part *spiritual.* The events are hard to understand because the spirit(s) stage-managing them are deliberately deceptive—*duplicitous*—to boot. Of course, this older formulation attributes to the 'managers' of these events deliberation and intentionality and a certain maliciousness, that is, *personality*.

But the archetypes with their 'surrounding' complexes *have* what Jung described as their own consciousness, along with an entire set (if somewhat stereotyped and one-dimensional) of attitudes, feelings, ideas and so forth—their own centres of personal identity. In short, each complex considers itself and behaves like a *being*. Jung claims that it is just when the archetypal (or instinctive) core of such a *'personified-complex'* is activated, that it produces 'parapsychological phenomena.'

Let us restate it without the scientisms. There exist invisible, incorporeal being-like entities with a semi-independent consciousness. Each has its own intentions, attitudes and feelings. Each can, it seems, 'possess' us and make us identify with what it wants. Such beings appear most readily when our instinctive cravings are activated. They seem able to provide us with information in a supernatural but most often in a frustratingly partial, hence useless, fashion. They are capable of moving objects around at a distance, often in a frightening, noisy, mischievous fashion just as if they take special pleasure in practical jokes.

If we de-sanitize the language, and restore the orthodox biblical symbol-system, we recognize 'activated archetypes generating parapsychological events' as a description of *demons*. For that is precisely what demons have always been thought to be: beings with their own intentions, duplicitous, tricky and *mercurial*, attachable in some way to the human mind, and appearing to feed upon unconstrained animal arousal; providing us with 'information', that is 'higher knowledge' which is a mixture of truth and falsehood.

In the section from his autobiography cited above, Jung goes on to explain how the figure of 'Elijah' in his visions, the prototype of the 'archetype of the Wise Old Man,' embodiment of 'knowledge and understanding'—but hardly the biblical Elijah!—mutates into another figure, also with a biblical name, but as with 'Elijah', bearing little resemblance to the original: Philemon.

Jung's Philemon was 'an old man with the horns of a bull...and the wings of a kingfisher.' He was lame, but represented for Jung 'spirit' and 'meaning' and 'superior insight.' He became Jung's spirit-guru, who taught him many things he himself did not know.

Though Jung did not explicitly draw the old folk connection between the horned, winged, lame 'Philemon,' and 'old lamefoot' (the devil), he notes that as 'Elijah' mutated into 'Philemon,' 'Philemon' later mutated into 'Ka,' an Egyptian 'earth-soul' that 'came from below.' He wrote:

> 'Ka's expression has something demonic about it, one might also say, Mephistophelian...In time, I was able to integrate both figures [Ka and Philemon] through the study of alchemy...'

whose presiding familiar spirit, we have already noted, is the two-faced *mercurius duplex*.

From this flux of demonic spirits arose the many mysterious 'parapsychological' phenomena that so enraptured Jung's Faustian intellect. From them as well he claimed to have learned much of his psychological theory and method, especially the technique of cultivating autonomous inner voices. During the period when his relationship with Freud was collapsing, and his personal visions began, he was much comforted, for a time, by the apparent affair he maintained with a brilliant and beautiful, but greatly troubled, Russian Jewish patient, from whom he continued to demand fees in spite of their liaison. Later, as he worked his way through alchemy and the Gnostics, his 'mystical sister' was yet another patient/lover with whom he and his wife maintained a decades-long *ménage à trois*. Thus we fall, as we make gods of our instincts, into the doctrines of demons:

> 'The Spirit clearly says that in later times some will abandon the faith and follow deceiving spirits and things taught by demons. Such teachings come through hypocritical liars, whose consciences have been seared as with a hot iron...Have nothing to do with godless myths and old wives tales; rather train yourself to be godly. For...godliness has value for all things, holding promise for both the present life and for the life to come.'
>
> (1 Timothy 4.1-10)